8 Realistic Track Plans

For Small Switching Layouts

By Lance Mindheim

CreateSpace.com

8 Realistic Track Plans

For Small Switching Layouts

Front Cover: The switcher for The Port of Palm Beach pulls a cut of container flats from the loading apron and hauls them the few blocks west to the Florida East Coast Railway interchange.

Back Cover: In this 2008 photo, the industrial local switches the Trujillo and Sons food warehouse in Miami, Florida.

Copyright 2009, Lance Mindheim

ISBN-13/EAN-13: 9781442176492

About The Author

Lance Mindheim is owner of The Shelf Layouts Company, a custom model railroad building and design firm. He speaks nationally at a variety of prototype modeling conferences and is author of numerous articles for the model railroad press. An engineering graduate of Purdue University, he is a strong believer in the value of simplicity when it comes to model railroad design. Visit his website at www.shelflayouts.com.

Table of Contents

Introduction

This scene from the author's layout is only 16" wide and illustrates what can be accomplished on a relatively narrow shelf.

Part of the appeal of model railroading is that there is no relationship between the size of the layout and the ultimate enjoyment it provides. Successful model railroads come in all sizes, each with their own pros and cons. Certainly large layouts have their advantages such as long mainline runs. However, smaller model railroads have their own positive attributes.

Small layouts can be built to higher levels of detail in shorter time periods. They require less maintenance and are less expensive. Then there is the obvious, they take up less space making them attainable to almost anybody regardless of their housing situation. Included in this book are eight plans of a size and complexity level within the reach of most modelers.

The plans are either directly tied to a specific railroad that actually exists (or existed) or are a composite of several actual railroads. They are designed to be

Small layouts can provide plenty of operational potential. Here, a two man crew switches a warehouse on the author's model railroad.

straightforward to build and enjoyable to operate. Small and simple does not mean un-sophisticated. Built with the proper level of care and attention, a completed version of any of these themes could be made into something that is a real attention getter.

Each plan has been prepared with realistic operations in mind. If the layouts are operated in the same manner, and with the same procedures as their real life counterparts, they can provide for many hours of relaxation after a hard day at work. The track arrangements have been prepared so that they can be operated efficiently and without frustrating, artificially inserted, 'switching puzzles'.

Depending on your interests and how long you plan on having the layout, you can decide on the level of finish appropriate for your situation. You could scratch build and super detail the project and stretch your construction enjoyment out for years if so desired. If you only plan on having the layout for a short period of time, you could simply employ commercial structures and be up a going in a matter of months. Small layouts offer a level of flexibility that puts you in charge of how far you want to take them. Let's turn the pages and look at some ideas.

The author's East Rail switching layout, shown above, floats off of the floor in such a way that there is minimal disruption to the rest of the room. The lighting valence serves the secondary purpose of reducing the amount of dust that falls on the layout.

Pull out drawers mounted into the fascia work well for car storage.

Some Construction Ideas

All of the plans in this book have the same bench work width of 18 inches. For those that employ staging cassettes, the cassette is 4 inches wide. A few designs have a small, double track, staging yard on one wall. In those cases, the width of the shelf for the small staging yard is 6 inches.

Standard bookshelf planks would work fine for the bench work slabs. Having said that, hollow core door blanks are less prone to warping and are relatively inexpensive. The door blanks can be cut to shorter lengths as necessary with a saw without compromising their integrity.

Most of the plans feature relatively flat scenery and there are no track grades. For your scenery base, simply take a piece of one-inch thick extruded foam insulation (the pink or blue stuff) and laminate it onto your door or shelf planks. To do this, cover your bench work surface with foam board adhesive, place the foam on top, weight the foam down, and allow it to dry overnight. Depending on the look you want, cork roadbed can be glued directly on top of the foam using yellow wood glue. If you want a shallower, more industrial looking roadbed, you can skip the cork entirely and lay your track directly on the foam. The foam can be carved and shaped into scenery contours easily with rasps, sand paper, and/or hot knife cutting tools.

To throw your turnouts (aka track switches) it is not necessary to go to the trouble to install switch machines. The trains are moving slowly and there is very little stress on the track. Simply flipping the turnout points with your fingertips will work. There is generally enough friction in the mechanism to keep the points in position. If the points seem loose, slipping a sliver of strip styrene under the throw rod will introduce enough friction to keep them securely in place. As far track goes, use a spacing of 2 inches between parallel track centers in HO scale. In cases where tracks parallel each other around a curve, increase the parallel spacing to 2 ½ inches so cars don't sideswipe one another.

All of the plans in this book are HO scale. However, they are easily adapted to N scale. One option would be to cut all of the dimensions in half and decrease your track centerline spacing from the HO distance of 2 inches to 1 inch for N scale. If you have the room, a better solution would be to leave all of the dimensions as is and just lay N scale track down over the same track centerlines as are shown for the HO designs (but again changing the parallel track spacing to 1 inch). Using the HO footprints for an N scale project will result in a very open, un-congested, attractive look. A CAD (computer-aided design) program was used to prepare the designs and actual track component dimensions used to ensure that the designs will actually fit as drawn.

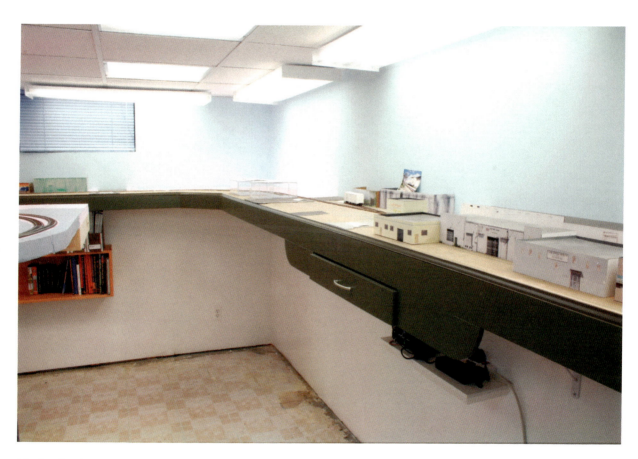

With a little extra effort a switching layout can be finished in such a way that it blends into a room attractively. In the photo above, floor trim molding was attached to the layout edge and painted a neutral green. Shelf brackets support the layout, making legs un-necessary, further adding to the open and clean look.

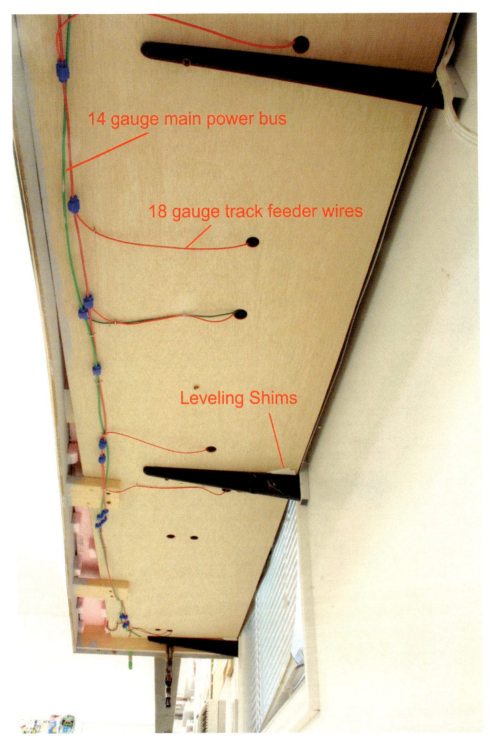

Shown here is an underside look at the bottom of a typical shelf mount, narrow width layout.

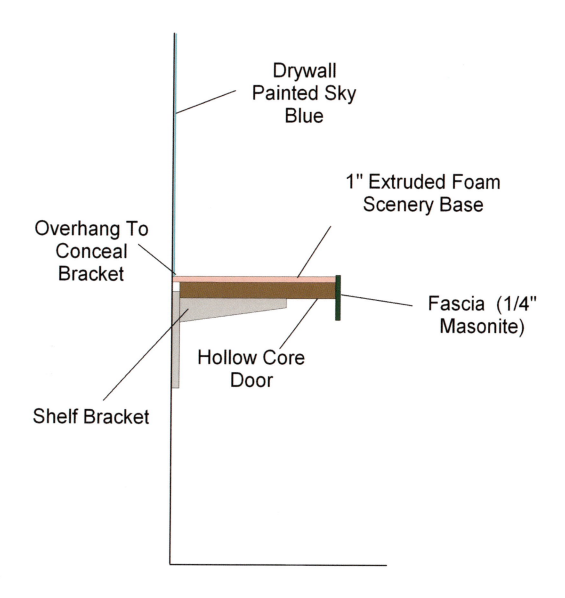

Drywall
Painted Sky
Blue

1" Extruded Foam
Scenery Base

Overhang To
Conceal
Bracket

Fascia (1/4"
Masonite)

Hollow Core
Door

Shelf Bracket

Hollow Core Bench
Work Detail

This side view illustrates common construction details for a shelf style bench work arrangement

Staging

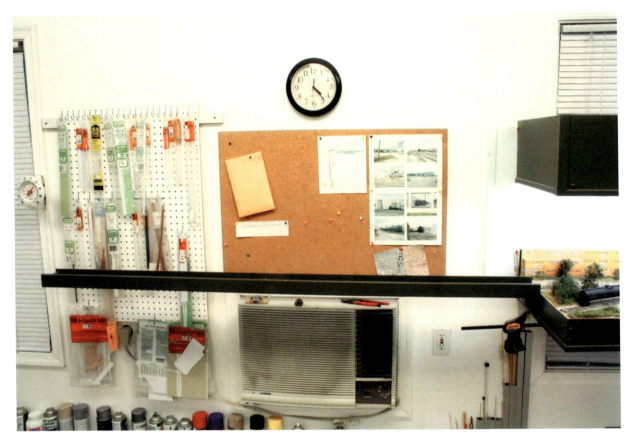

Simple, removable staging cassettes can be set aside out of the way when the railroad is not in use.

On small switching layouts, employing staging yards to represent the outside world is less of an issue than with larger layouts. In most cases, only a single train is on the layout at a time and the length of that train is relatively short. Even so, it is handy to have a longer stretch of tail track leading into the layout. Since this tail track (or mini-staging track) often blocks surrounding doors, and is only needed during operating sessions, it is helpful to make it removable. The solution is a simple 'staging cassette'. The cassette is no more than a simple 1"x4" piece of lumber with some flex track laid on it. The sides of the cassette can be built up with molding to improve the appearance and to provide guardrails. Support is provided by clamping the cassette to the layout at one end and by a short shelf bracket at the other. Power is provided through banana plugs or simply through the rail joiners used to join the staging cassette to the layout.

The Room

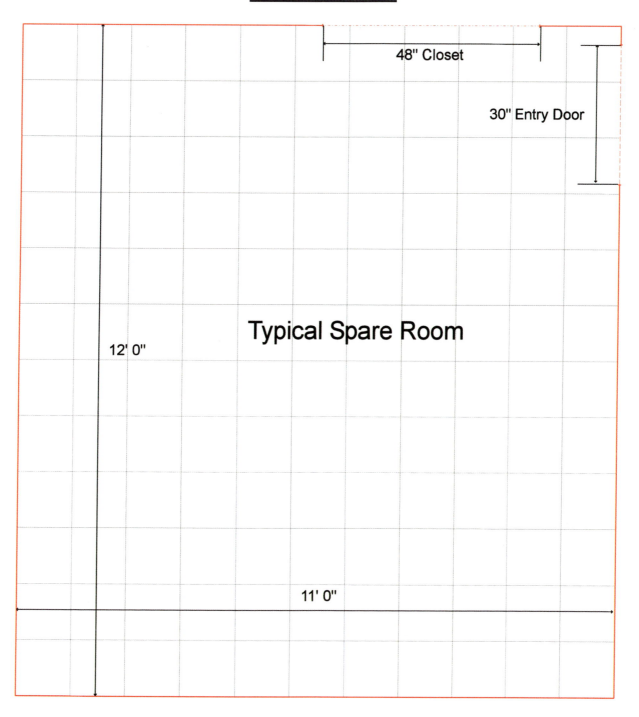

All of the designs in this book assume that the layout is placed in a typical spare room with the dimensions shown above. These dimensions were taken from an actual room in my house and should be representative of the space many people have available to work with.

Port of Palm Beach

You won't find many paint schemes like that found on the Port of Palm Beach switcher shown above! I've heard various stories related to the origin of the theme including one that it is a 9/11 remembrance.

It's hard to deny the appeal of any layout featuring rail/marine operations. There is something irresistible about the process of transferring cargo from the rails to a seagoing vessel. While many modern era ports are so large that modeling them would be difficult, the Port of Palm Beach in Riviera Beach, Florida is an exception. It's only a few blocks long and relatively short cargo ships still call there. The Port of Palm Beach's motive power consists of a single switcher decked out in a distinctive red, white, and blue paint scheme. Connection to the outside world is through an interchange track linked to the Florida East Coast main that runs behind the port.

Despite its small size, the railroad handles a diverse group of commodities including: break bulk cargoes, sugar, molasses, cement, water, utility fuels, and produce. Although the track plan here represents the port in its modern form, operations date back to the 1900's and there is no reason something from an earlier era couldn't be modeled.

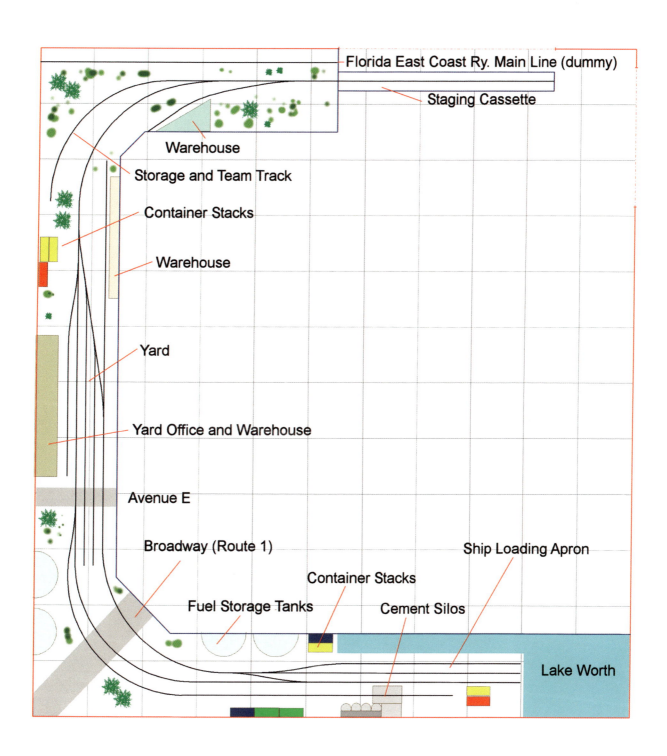

Florida East Coast Ry. Main Line (dummy)

Staging Cassette

Warehouse

Storage and Team Track

Container Stacks

Warehouse

Yard

Yard Office and Warehouse

Avenue E

Broadway (Route 1)

Ship Loading Apron

Container Stacks

Fuel Storage Tanks

Cement Silos

Lake Worth

Name: Port of Palm Beach	
Era: Present	
Bench Work Width: 18"	
Staging Cassette Width: 4"	
Flex Track Quantity: 85 feet	
Curve Radius: 27"	
Turnout Quantity:	
Number 6 Left (5),	Number 6 Right (5)

Heading westbound, the switcher pulls a cut of cars towards Avenue E. Route 1 passes above in the distance.

Having just been offloaded from a ship onto container flats, two Tropical Shipping containers are shuttled to the Florida East Coast Railway interchange track.

Operations for the Port of Palm Beach Railroad are housed in the structure shown above. In addition to the railroad's office, the building serves double duty as a warehouse.

Looking east from Avenue E, the switcher can be seen in the distance at its typical parking place under the Route 1 overpass. When a call comes into the crew that a switching move is needed, they load into a golf cart and drive it from the office down to the switcher!

In the above photo, facing west, the Port's tracks curve to the north where they meet with the Florida East Coast main.

Directly across the yard from the yard office is a warehouse. In this view, the spur is probably serving as an overflow storage track instead of as a warehouse lead.

Container storage yards such this surround the port.

Modern Industrial Park

In this 2008 photo, the industrial local switches a food warehouse in Miami, Florida.

Modern era industrial parks have appeal on several fronts. First, the rail operations involved in switching them are very much the same as earlier eras and are therefore just as interesting to perform. Unlike earlier era's, however, modern industrial parks have the added advantage that you are able to visit them, take photographs, and study them. The following track plan is a composite of industrial parks in several locations: Beltsville MD, Rockville, MD, South Bend, IN and Miami, FL.

The freight car roster needed to serve a layout such as this would be diverse and include: LPG tank cars, plastic pellet hoppers, boxcars, gondola's, coke hoppers, chemical tank cars, and anything required at the team track. When switching the warehouse, remember that the plant foreman will want the cars spotted at specific doors. When delivering a car to the team track, make sure you have the appropriate unloading equipment, such as a cherry picker or pneumatic trailer, at the ready to handle unloading.

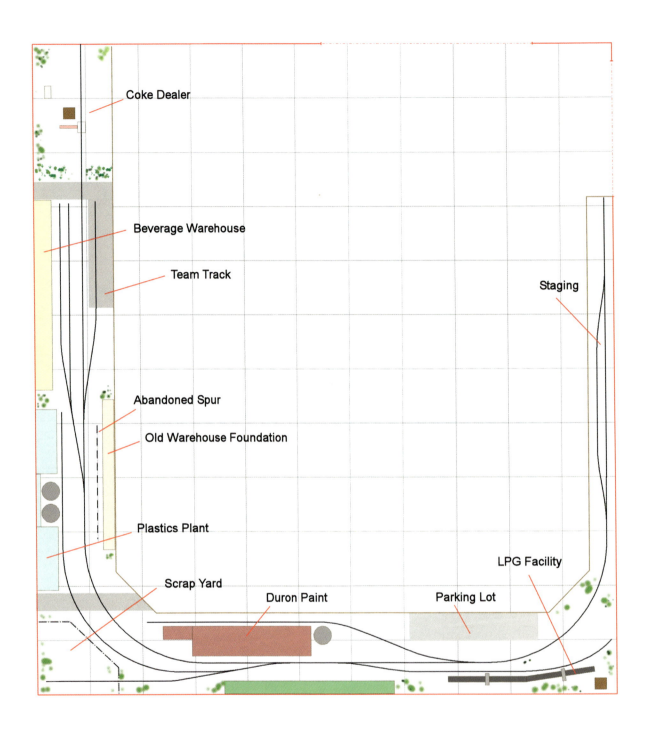

Coke Dealer

Beverage Warehouse

Team Track

Staging

Abandoned Spur

Old Warehouse Foundation

Plastics Plant

LPG Facility

Scrap Yard

Duron Paint

Parking Lot

Name: Modern Industrial Park

Era: Present

Bench Work Width: 18"

Staging Bench Work Width: 6"

Flex Track Quantity: 64 feet

Curve Radius: 27"

Turnout Quantity:

  Number 6 Left (3),   Number 6 Right (6)

Tonawanda Coke. South Bend, IN 2009

Weeks Gas (LPG). Miami, FL 2006

Team track. Rockville, MD 2006

Scrap Dealer, Miami, FL 2006

Alcoholic beverage warehouse. Derwood, Maryland.

Duron Paint. Beltsville, Maryland

Both of these photos were taken along Orange Avenue in Orlando, Florida in early 2005. In the top photo, the local switches out a warehouse. The bottom image is of a scrap yard with the rail spur barely visible in the distance.

Gotham City Freight House

In the years prior to the days of FedEx and UPS, packages far too small to warrant their own boxcar were grouped with like packages and moved by rail. Called less than carload, or lcl for short, your typical Sears and Roebuck order would be dropped at a freight house, grouped with other small packages heading in the same direction, and loaded into clean boxcars. In larger cities such as Chicago, New York, or Philadelphia the freight houses were massive and their traffic movements complex. Cuts of empty cars would be spotted at the platforms in the morning for loading. A designated cut off time would be set for getting the outbound cars loaded. When the cutoff time arrived, the car doors were closed, the cars picked up by a switcher and taken to the yard so they could be blocked into the appropriate manifest freight in time for its scheduled departure.

The Gotham City freight plan provides a means of reliving this fascinating freight house activity from 1940's and early 1950's. A typical operating session would begin in the yard with the switcher blocking a string of cars to be taken to the freight house. Within the block of cars would be inbound loads to be spotted at one platform (or even specific door) for unloading as well as empties to be delivered for loading. Later in your operating session you will need to pick up the cars that were loaded at the freight house, bring them back to the yard, and re-block them so they can be taken out on the appropriate mainline fast freight.

In addition to the freight house facility, the plan includes a cold storage and produce warehouse for reefer traffic. There is also a team track that could handle almost any type of car type as well as a coal yard for hoppers.

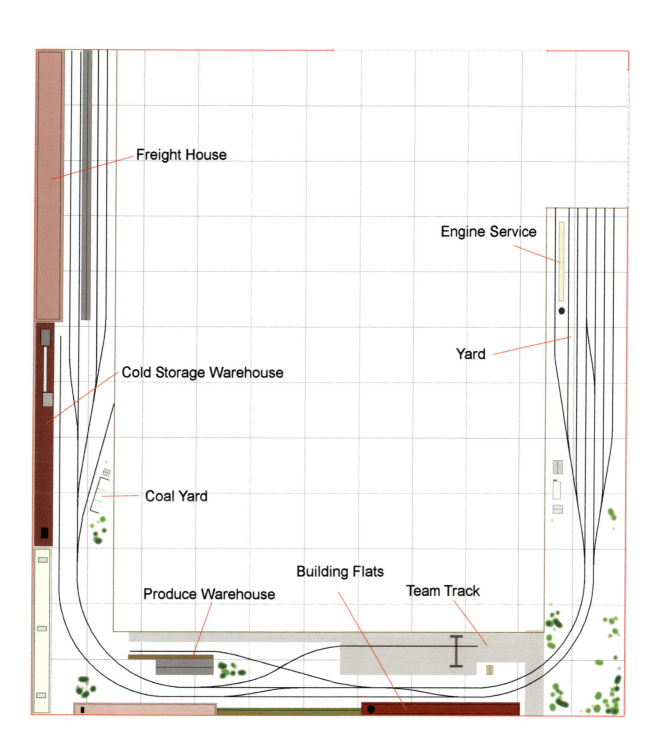

Freight House

Engine Service

Cold Storage Warehouse

Yard

Coal Yard

Building Flats

Produce Warehouse

Team Track

Name: Gotham City Freight House
Era: 1942 - 1955
Bench Work Width: 18"
Flex Track Quantity: 100 feet
Curve Radius: 24"
Turnout Quantity: Number 6 Left (9),   Number 6 Right (8)
Crossings: 45 degree

There are number of suitable kits on the market that can be easily kitbashed into your typical imposing, blocks long, freight house. The freight house in the photos above was constructed by stitching several Walthers kits together.

Prairie Branch Line

This Farmersville, Illinois elevator illustrates the endless variety seen in these 'Prairie Skyscrapers'.

Depending how you define it, the American 'Prairie' could be viewed as extending from Ohio to as far west as Montana. Often flat as a pool table and covered with oceans of crop fields, the prairie is home to an endless count of small towns each with its own set of industries needing rail service.

At first glance, many of these small towns would appear to have the same industries. Grain elevators, fuel dealers, and lumberyards seem to be everywhere. A closer look, however, reveals that no two grain elevators, or any industry for that matter, are exactly the same.

The Prairie Branch Line represents a series of tiny villages, with populations likely no larger than several hundred people strung side by side along the line like pearls on a necklace.

A typical operating session would start with a short freight staged on the cassette with a half dozen cars and a caboose. It's assumed that that the way freight is midway down some mythical branch when the session starts. The train arrives at Town B and slowly goes about its work of switching the local grain elevators and industries. Switching the furniture factory would likely take more time as the crew makes sure each car is spotted at the correct location in front of the plant. Finally, the train stops in front of the depot to pick up any small packages that might get loaded into a dedicated clean boxcar spotted behind the engine.

Leaving Town B in the rearview mirror, the train crosses the corn or wheat fields until it arrives at Town A to perform similar tasks. At Town A, the branch line interchanges with a major class 1 road where cars will be picked up and set out. When the work at Town A is done, the engine runs around its train and heads back towards staging.

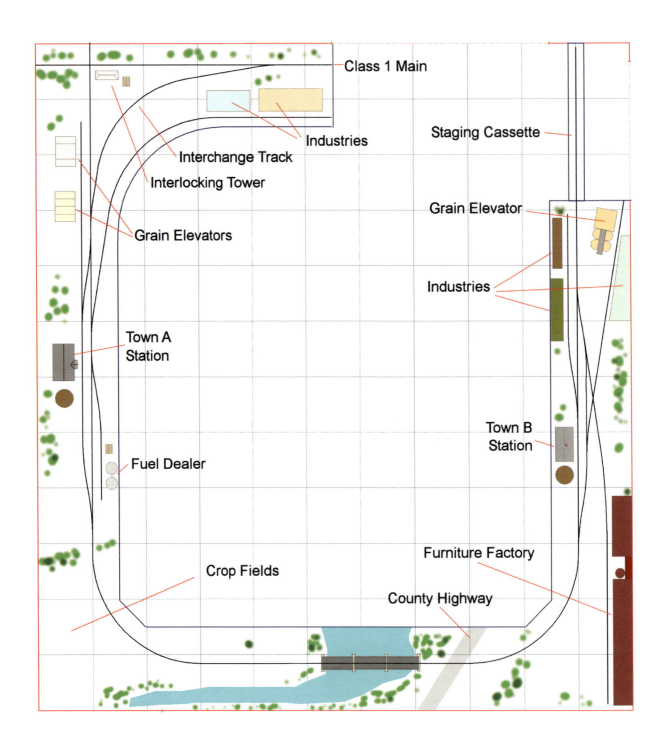

Class 1 Main

Industries

Staging Cassette

Interchange Track

Interlocking Tower

Grain Elevator

Grain Elevators

Industries

Town A
Station

Town B
Station

Fuel Dealer

Furniture Factory

Crop Fields

County Highway

Name: Prairie Branch Line

Era: 1940 - 1960

Bench Work Width: 18"

Staging Cassette Width: 4"

Flex Track Quantity: 65 feet

Curve Radius: 24"

Turnout Quantity:

Number 6 Left (5),   Number 6 Right (7)

Grain elevators in Farmersville, Illinois.

Pennsylvania RR, Delmarva Peninsula

Art rendition of the Pennsylvania Railroad Station in Cambridge, Maryland.

The Pennsylvania Railroad's branch line network once spread over the Delmarva Peninsula like branches from a tree. More often than not, one of those branches would make an abrupt dead end stop at the point where the rails met the Chesapeake Bay. Villages such as Cambridge, Crisfield, and St. Michaels, with all of their dilapidated wooden seafood plants and quaint stations, would make the mouth of a craftsman structure modeler drool. While fishing may have been the signature industry of such towns, the population at large had the needs of any other place in the country. That being the case, the railroads also served the town's coal and fuel dealers, grain elevators, warehouses, and lumberyards.

This particular track plan is patterned largely after Cambridge, MD. Although condominium development is beginning to take its toll on history, enough of the original structures still stand that a visitor to Cambridge can still easily get a sense for what once was.

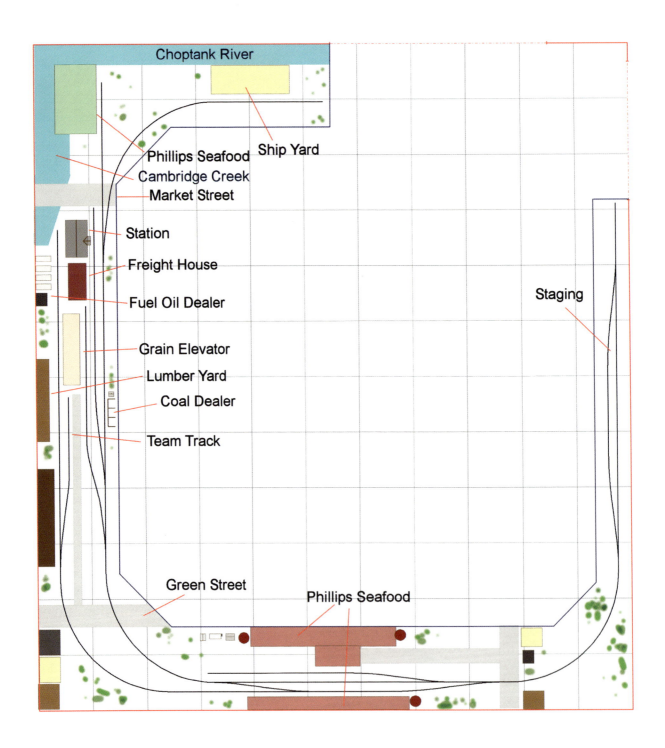

Choptank River

Phillips Seafood

Ship Yard

Cambridge Creek

Market Street

Station

Freight House

Fuel Oil Dealer

Grain Elevator

Lumber Yard

Coal Dealer

Team Track

Staging

Green Street

Phillips Seafood

Name: Pennsylvania RR, Delmarva Peninsula
Era: 1940- 1959
Bench Work Width: 18"
Staging Bench Work Width: 8"
Flex Track Quantity: 60 feet
Curve Radius: 24"
Turnout Quantity: Number 6 Left (4),   Number 6 Right (6)

Further reading: "A Branch Line Odyssey". Frank Donovan. Trains Magazine. May 1947.

The Pennsy Station in Cambridge, MD was still in excellent condition and serving as a real estate office when this photo was taken in 1999.

Oil dealer (top two photos). Grain elevator (bottom photo).

The top two photos are of the remnants of the once massive Phillips Seafood factory. The bottom photo is of what I believe was once a ship or boat building facility.

New York Dock Railway

Fulton Terminal

It would be hard to find a rail/marine enthusiast that doesn't own a copy of Thomas Flagg's Book 'New York Harbor Railroads in Color' (Morning Sun Books). What makes the small railroads that used to surround New York harbor so unique, and thus begging to be modeled, is their complete isolation. Unlike most areas of the country where even the smallest short line has at least one direct link to another railroad, the harbor railroads were completely cut off. Shoehorned between the harbor or river on one side and urban landscape on the other, the only connection the dock railroads had to the rest of the rail network was via car float. A typical New York harbor railroad would cover just a few square blocks. Within that several block area would be tight clusters of warehouses and team tracks served by track with the tightest of curves. The harbor roads all had one thing in common though, the car floats that provided a connection to the outside world.

In Volume 1, Flagg documents the New York Dock Railway's Fulton Terminal tucked under a freeway and jutting out just far enough to touch the water. It was a railroad that would have been easy to miss if your weren't looking for it. Those that did stumble upon it though were rewarded by the sight of tangerine and white GE 50 ton locomotives creeping out from their rabbit hole under the freeway to meet an arriving car float. After unloading the float, the rolling stock would be distributed to the industries in the several acre area surrounding the float operation. Car traffic flowed both ways and empties would be picked up, loaded back on the float, and sent back to their home road.

If one were to build this layout, the Walthers car float model could be used. Micro Engineering has a viaduct system that would serve as a good starting point for the freeway. A number of manufacturers, including DPM and Walthers, have kits that would be suitable for the warehouses.

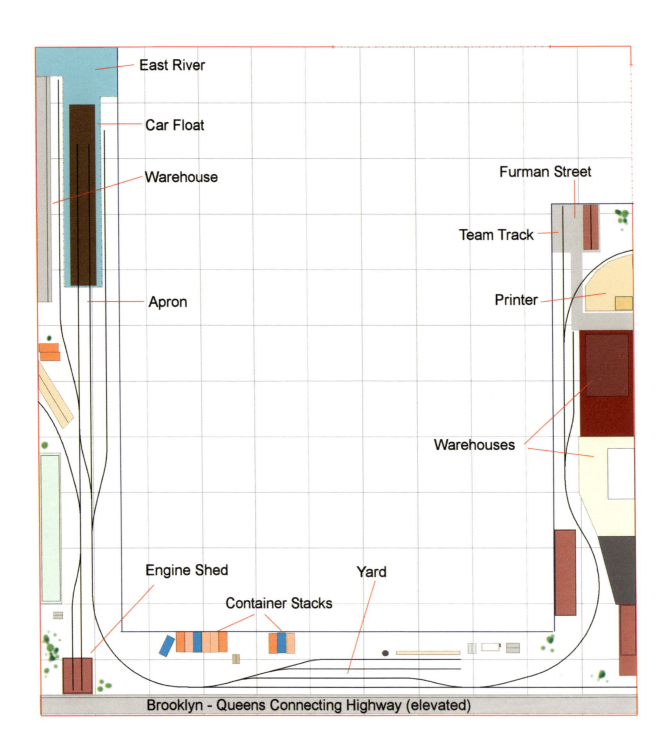

East River

Car Float

Warehouse

Furman Street

Team Track

Apron

Printer

Warehouses

Engine Shed

Yard

Container Stacks

Brooklyn - Queens Connecting Highway (elevated)

Name: New York Dock Railway – Fulton Terminal

Era: 1960 -1980

Bench Work Width: 18"

Flex Track Quantity: 68 feet

Curve Radius: 20"

Turnout Quantity:

Number 4 Left (6),   Number 4 Right (4)

Monon Railroad, Bloomington, Indiana

In this view from the 1930's, a load of furnaces is being unloaded at the team track platform adjacent to the Monon Railroad's Bloomington, Indiana freight house. The view is facing northeast with Fifth Street just behind the boxcar. (Photo courtesy of the Monroe County, Indiana Historical Society)

Bloomington, Indiana in the 1940's and 1950's was Mainstreet, USA. With a population during that period around 20,000, it was typical of hundreds, if not thousands, of mid-sized towns throughout the country. The Monon Railroad sliced right through the center of town with industries tightly packed a block to each side of the rail corridor. Paralleling the track was a diverse blend of coal yards, fuel oil dealers, lumberyards, a creamery, a grain elevator, and grocery wholesalers.

The design for this Bloomington based layout focuses on accurately modeling the one-mile stretch of track between the Monon Railroad's McDoel Yard and downtown. The industries featured in the design actually existed and they are drawn in the same relative locations as they appeared in real life.

To operate the layout, the local switch job would begin on the staging cassette which serves as a stand-in for McDoel yard. Either the yard job powered by an NW2, or a northbound local featuring an RS-2, would handle the switching chores. The train would proceed northward from staging into town to switch the various industries. Historic aerial photos indicate that the small yard at the freight house was generally packed with cars. That being the case, the local had its work cut out for it as it switched the freight house swapping loads and empties. Outbound loaded cars leaving the freight house had to be delivered back to the yard in time to make the cut off for the next manifest freight. As the layout is switched, the operator will need to make sure that the grade crossings aren't blocked. The runaround will have to be utilized to handle the facing point switches. All totaled, this design makes for an interesting operating scenario that will keep several modelers fully occupied.

This aerial photo, taken by the author in the early 1970's, shows the Monon Railroad right-of-way slicing through downtown Bloomington, Indiana.

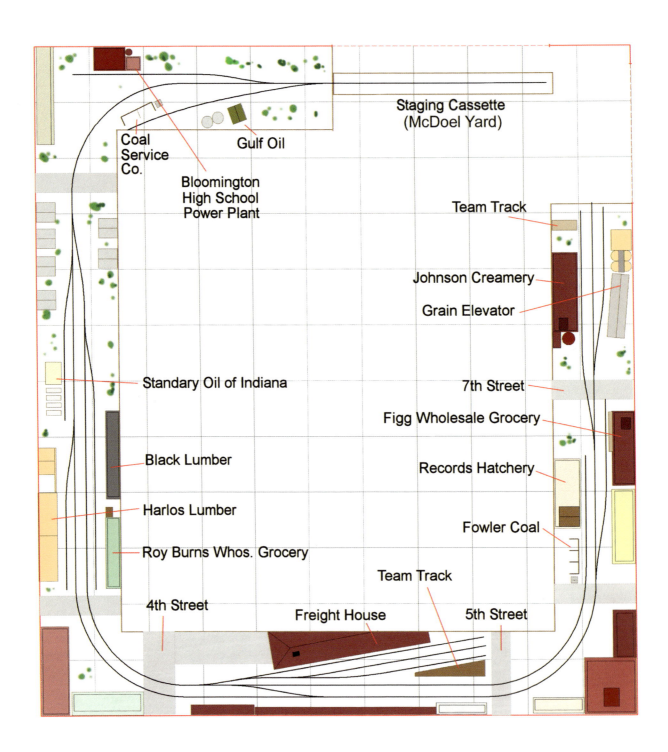

Coal
Service
Co.

Gulf Oil

Staging Cassette
(McDoel Yard)

Bloomington
High School
Power Plant

Team Track

Johnson Creamery

Grain Elevator

Standary Oil of Indiana

7th Street

Figg Wholesale Grocery

Black Lumber

Records Hatchery

Harlos Lumber

Fowler Coal

Roy Burns Whos. Grocery

Team Track

4th Street

Freight House

5th Street

Name: Monon RR, Bloomington, Indiana

Era: 1945 - 1955

Bench Work Width: 18"

Staging Cassette Width: 4"

Flex Track Quantity: 90 feet

Curve Radius: 24"

Turnout Quantity:

  Number 6 Left (5),   Number 6 Right (8)

The original J.R. Figg Wholesale Grocer structure still stands and is now an antique mall.

The Johnson's Creamery structure, with its landmark stack, has been preserved and restored.

Standard Oil of Indiana

The Beginner

The 'Beginner' is designed to be a practice layout with the purpose of developing basic construction skills. It takes up very little space and would be relatively inexpensive to build. Even in the tightest of quarters, most people can free up the room for a bookshelf size run such as this along one wall.

Despite its small size, however, there is still plenty of potential for operational fun. At one end is a small yard where cars can be sorted, blocked, and made into trains for transfer runs to the other end of the layout. Upon leaving the yard, the switcher can lazily work away spotting cars at the various industries.

Name: The Beginner	
Era: Any	
Bench Work Width: 18"	
Flex Track Quantity: 30 feet	
Curve Radius: n/a	
Turnout Quantity:	
Number 6 Left (5),	Number 6 Right (5)

Team
Track

Atlas Lumber
Yard

Warehouse

Fuel
Oil Dealer

Depot &
Freight House

Yard

Engine Service

<u>Parting Thoughts</u>

The yard job, Y120 wraps up a day of work on the author's East Rail layout. The bench work is roughly 21" at this end of the layout.

Model railroad's need not be large, complicated, or expensive in order to provide a tremendous amount of enjoyment. The model railroads in this book would easily fit into a spare bedroom, a study, or corner of a basement. These small layouts could serve strictly as a training exercise without involving a lot of expense. On the flip side of the coin, a small switching layout could be covered with handcrafted, scratch-built structures, and super detailed in a such a way that it would grab anybody's attention.   They are extremely versatile and, as mentioned before in the book, are suitable for anybody from a teenager just starting out in the hobby to the most experienced of modeling craftsman.

Other Books By Lance Mindheim

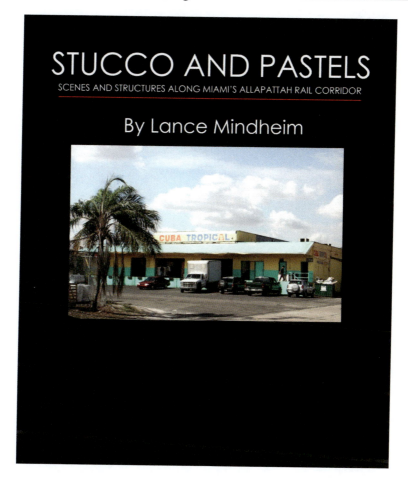

Stucco and Pastels takes you on a walk through America's Casablanca. The landscape surrounding a little known railroad branch running through Miami's Allapattah neighborhood is rich in images typically associated with bygone days. Follow along as this photo documentary walks you through images of faded pastel art deco structures, narrow avenues draped with umbrellas of palmetto palms, and romantic maritime scenes.

Made in the USA
Lexington, KY
15 November 2013